THIS IS A TEST

A Handbook for
Writing Good Tests

JAN GLEITER

🍎 Maupin House by
capstone·
professional

This Is a Test:
A Handbook for Writing Good Tests
By Jan Gleiter

Cover Design: Sarah Bennett
Book Design: Sarah Bennett

Image Credits:
Shutterstock: studioVin, cover (pencil), Inna Astakhova, cover (wood background)

Library of Congress Cataloging-in-Publication Data
Gleiter, Jan, 1947-
  This is a test : a handbook for writing good tests / by Jan Gleiter.
     pages cm
  ISBN 978-1-62521-514-7 (pb)
  1. Educational tests and measurements—Design and construction. 2.
Examinations—Design and construction. I. Title.
  LB3051.G533 2013
  371.26—dc23   2013036513

Maupin House publishes professional resources for K–12 educators. Contact us for
tailored, in-school training or to schedule an author for a workshop or conference.
Visit www.maupinhouse.com for free lesson plan downloads.

Maupin House Publishing, Inc. by Capstone Professional

1710 Roe Crest Drive
North Mankato, MN 56003
www.maupinhouse.com
888-262-6135
info@maupinhouse.com

10 9 8 7 6 5 4 3 2 1

Printed in the United States of America in Eau Claire, Wisconsin.
112013   007880

For my mother, Marcia Gleiter, who was not just a wonderful mother but who taught me the beauty of clear language and the power of words. As a teacher, she would have liked this book, or so I sincerely hope.

Some books may spring entirely from their author's minds. This one most certainly did not, and I want to thank just a few of the people who helped me along the way. First, it was Ruth and Walter MacGinitie who awakened my interest in testing and who taught me much about the multiple-choice item and the extraordinary importance of validity. In addition, I would like to thank Kate Montgomery for her invaluable encouragement, Kathleen Thompson for the usefulness of her suggestions regarding organization and for taking a chance on me, my sister Karin for proofreading, Afrodite Barz for letting me do my job my way, and Greg Pierce for going beyond our professional relationship in his suggestions and help. Lastly, thanks to my wonderful husband Paul Thompson, who took on more than his fair share while I was writing.

TABLE OF CONTENTS

FOREWORD

What a good book this is! Some handbooks lie dormant on the shelf, some deservedly so. But not so with this one. Jan Gleiter's short, commonsensical approach provides much-needed clarity to the oft-overlooked task of test construction at all grade levels. Through generous helpings of flawed and valid examples of questions and their answers, Gleiter gently guides readers through familiar territory, causing us to see testing in a new light.

Her keen sense of humor and elegant prose make this a must-read and a must-reread for both novice and expert test developers. I suspect the "Aha" moments will occur at different places with each read.

The 15 rules of good test writing unfold naturally as Gleiter narrates her story of the what, when, why, and how of different types of test items. The final chapter provides not just a summary but also a hands-on exercise to help ensure that what remains in the minds of readers is not inert knowledge but ready-to-use skills. *This Is a Test* is a test worth taking.

Vincent L. Cyboran, Ed.D.
Graduate Program in Training and Development
Roosevelt University
Chicago, Illinois

INTRODUCTION

There are other ways to assess students, employees, job applicants, and candidates for medical research besides giving them a traditional pencil-and-paper or computer-and-mouse test. In a school setting, these other ways are generally termed "alternative assessment" and include portfolios, interviews, journals, and learning logs, as well as that time-honored method known as "observation." I'm going to assume you know about them. Despite the usefulness of these other methods, many people rely, for a variety of reasons, on pencil-and-paper tests. (I'm going to drop the "pencil-and-paper" modifier from here on out. For the rest of this handbook, when I use the word test, I don't mean performance test, laboratory test, lie detector test, or "If your mother and I both fell overboard, whom would you save first?" test. I mean pencil-and-paper test.)

In the real life that whirls around us, tests are almost nonexistent except in one's attempts to acquire various kinds of licenses. What people know and how well they know it is rarely determined through testing. It is determined by discussion and observation. Testing is an imperfect substitute for discussion and observation. All tests are imperfect substitutes.

How many times, in a conversation, have you asked a question, listened to a person begin to answer you, and then interrupted with "No, I meant…"? This is not possible during a test.

How many times, in a conversation, have you asked a question, listened to the answer, and realized that you needed to follow up with another, more specific, question to get the information you were really after? This is not possible during a test.

How many times, in a conversation, have you asked a question based on an assumption, listened to the reply, and realized that your assumption was wrong? This is not possible during a test.

How many times have you wondered how good someone is at something and found out by watching? This is not possible during a test.

If teachers had time to carry on searching conversations with each student and observe those things that can't be discussed, they probably wouldn't use tests any more than parents, friends, and shift supervisors do. Time restrictions make this impossible and make testing necessary. The purpose of this handbook is to make tests less imperfect substitutes—to help those people, particularly teachers, who want or need to write tests to write better ones.

Why Give Tests at All?

There are many reasons to give tests. They may not be the best way to determine what, or how much, someone knows or can do, but they are often the best practical way. They are useful for answering questions you have about your students. How much do they know? Or what skills have they mastered? Or how closely have they listened to all those brilliant things you've been saying? Or do they stand a chance of passing the state-mandated test you'll be administering in a few weeks? A good test will help you answer your question. A bad test may help you answer some other question, but you may never know what question that was.

In addition to helping you answer questions you have about your students, good tests actually help students learn. They encourage students to study the material they've been assigned. They provide a way for students to measure their own progress. And, if a test is reviewed after being returned to the class, with discussions about why the keyed (correct) answers are actually correct and the distractors (incorrect answers) are actually incorrect, it can serve as a solid review.

Reviewing essay tests can also be helpful. Without identifying the students who wrote them, you could read aloud the best answers or several very good answers you received, identifying what was insightful or meaningful about them. (If you didn't receive any very good answers, perhaps you were asking for information or interpretations that your students didn't have the necessary basis for answering.)

Preparing for High Stakes Tests

Another reason to give tests is to prepare your students for statewide and national tests. Although many statewide tests in the past have left a lot to be desired in terms of validity and reliability, the new tests aligned with the Common Core State Standards (CCSS) are virtually guaranteed to be significantly better and significantly harder. If your students are not used to valid tests with good distractors, they will be mystified when presented with one.

Take distractors, for example. (See Rule 6 on page 37 and the copy that follows it.) Students who are not used to dealing with well-written distractors will think a test that contains them is trying to trick them, which will frustrate them and increase their test anxiety. Distractors are meant to distract the *unknowing* examinee. Unfortunately, they can distract the knowing examinee if that examinee is confused by the idea of answer choices that are appealing. If students are used to dealing with good distractors, they will have a significant advantage over students who are not. Likewise, students who are not used to dealing with challenging tests will give up quickly when faced with one. On the other hand, students who have consistently been presented with fair, challenging, well-constructed, valid tests will take high-stakes tests in their stride.

You owe it to your students to consistently present them with such tests. They will not only tell you what you need to know about your students' understanding of the material you've been teaching, but they also will prepare your students for high-stakes tests.

Why Bad Tests Matter

If teachers were, and they are, as concerned with ethics as medical students, they too would learn the phrase, "First, do no harm." Bad tests do harm.

If the alternative to good tests were no tests at all, education would survive. Teachers would find other ways of measuring progress and mastery. Unfortunately, the alternative to good tests is, almost always, bad tests. And bad tests have bad consequences. The consequences range from the inconvenient and troublesome to the downright disastrous. For one thing, they tend to teach poor learning habits and make students feel that there is no point in studying or learning.

Bad tests differ from each other in innumerable ways, but they share one characteristic: They are invalid. They do not measure what they are intended to measure. As a result, they lead to erroneous conclusions.

Teachers who *know* that they don't know whether a student has mastered a skill or learned a subject will pay attention to what the student says and does. They will notice indications of mastery or lack of it. Teachers who *think they know but are wrong* are far less likely to notice such indications.

Teachers are likely to receive ready-made tests as part of program materials. If a particular test that you've been given to administer is flawed, you could choose not to administer it unless it is a mandated test. Even in those situations in which you believe a test is flawed but must administer it, you can avoid basing your own teaching on the scores your students receive. If you don't know you're administering a bad test, face it, you're going to come to erroneous conclusions. And you will believe your conclusions are accurate.

In addition to leading teachers to erroneous conclusions, bad tests are confusing to those who take them. They can create panic, frustration, and cynicism in students, and these reactions can have significant and long-lasting effects. Students who have negative associations with testing tend to do poor on tests, even good tests.

Children are not born with test anxiety. Tell any 4-year-old child that you want to find out how much he or she knows about something, and the child is almost certain to react with curiosity and eagerness. It's all just another game, and children tend to want to prove just how knowledgeable they are. However, if we give children enough bad tests, they are almost guaranteed to develop test anxiety, and test anxiety can have terrible consequences: lowered scores, more self-image problems, and less accurate expectations of how much they can learn.

In test development, there is no substitute for common sense. The rules for test writing provide a jumping-off place; any test written in accordance with the rules will be better than any test not written in accordance with them. That does not mean that the result will be a good test.

For a test to be good, the writer must have engaged his or her brain. Fully. And he or she must have consistently paid attention to what is possible, reasonable, and fair. Are you testing what you think you are testing? Are you testing what you claim you are testing? Most important, if there is another, better way to determine what you want to know, forget the test and use that other method! If not, follow the 15 rules in this book and write a good test.

ASSESSMENT LINGO

It will be easier to discuss testing if a few of the most common terms are understood. Here they are, in no particular order:

examinee: Someone taking a test.

item: A test question with its answer choices.

stem: The question part of an item. This can be "complete," which means it ends with a question mark, or "incomplete," which means it is a statement to be completed by selecting one of the answer choices.

distractor: (or *distracter*) An incorrect answer choice, so named for a reason. A distractor is meant to appeal to (or "distract") the examinee who doesn't know the answer. (It should never distract any examinee by taking his or her mind off the issue or fact being assessed.) That is, incorrect answers should appeal to examinees who do not have the knowledge or skill that the item requires.

keyed response: The answer choice the test developers have determined is correct. The keyed response is, ideally, the same thing as the correct response.

selected response: Any test item for which the examinee chooses an answer from an array of choices. The most common type of selected-response item is multiple-choice, but true/false and matching items are also "selected response."

constructed response: Any item for which the examinee must construct, rather than select, an answer. These include fill-in-the-blank items as well as both short-response items and essay questions.

chance factor: The mathematical chance that an answer choice selected randomly will be correct. In a multiple-choice item with four possible answers, the chance factor is 25 percent; with five answer choices, the chance factor is 20 percent.

p-value: The percentage of examinees who choose the keyed response to an item. Easy tests have many items with high p-values; hard tests have many items with low p-values. The p-value for any item on a test must be significantly higher than the chance factor for that item. This means that a typical multiple-choice item with four answer choices must have a p-value of more than 25.

validity: A test is valid if it measures what it purports to measure. For a test to be valid, its items must be valid. Anything that interferes with accurate measurement creates problems of invalidity. For example, an item meant to measure mastery of a particular skill is invalid if it also requires mastery of another skill— because one cannot tell which skill was lacking in the examinee who answered it incorrectly.

reliability: A test is reliable if it consistently ranks examinees in the same way. That is, if a test were given that ranked the examinees in a particular order and then given again to the same examinees and ranked them in a different order, that test is unreliable. If two tests were given to the same examinees, each test intended to measure the same knowledge or ability, and the two tests produced very different results, one or both of the tests would be unreliable. An example of an unreliable test is one that is extremely easy or extremely hard because chance would play such a large role in determining the results. Any test that has ambiguous items or unclear essay questions will be unreliable since the way the examinees understand the questions is what is being tested rather than the examinees' actual knowledge or ability.

CHAPTER 1

WHY WRITE THE TEST YOURSELF?

Sometimes you don't have any choice but to write a test yourself. College professors usually design their own programs, and many elementary and high-school teachers do too. If you've designed your own program, you're going to have to write your own tests. Even if you're using a purchased program or a basal text that came with a test booklet, the tests in it may not meet your needs. Assume for the moment that the tests you received are good. This doesn't mean that they meet your needs. They may be chapter tests, but you want unit tests, or they may be unit tests when you want chapter tests. They may include essay questions that you don't have time to grade. They may be harder than you want your tests to be. They may not take your students' reading difficulties into account. In these and other cases, you're going to need to write your own.

The next time you review a program you're thinking of using or you've been told to use, look at the tests. Look closely at the tests. Start by looking at the questions—the scope of them, the way they are worded, the demands they make, the assumptions they make, and how clear they are. Take one of the tests. Go on, be an examinee. Take a test. Then look at the answer key. If the test is a good one, it will be apparent to you. If you find it doesn't meet your needs, revise the test for your students.

Even if the existing tests are just dandy for your purposes, matched to your students' abilities, and reflective of your own teaching philosophy, there are still good reasons to write your own. Writing your own tests will help you teach better. Writing a draft of your test before you begin teaching the material will help you identify what you want and expect students to learn.

This is, after all, what you will put on your test. Such a process can only help to focus your teaching. (Before administering the test, you can revise it to reflect what you have found yourself emphasizing while teaching.)

Tests you have written yourself can also be indicative of how well you're teaching. If a goodly percentage of your students do well on a test you wrote yourself, one that reflects what you think you taught them, you probably did teach those things. If few do well, you might want to think about how you're presenting the information.

For whatever reason you find yourself in the situation of writing a test, it isn't the worst thing that ever happened to a teacher. It isn't even in the top 100. Or it doesn't need to be.

One of the nice things about developing tests is that the rules for writing good ones are all quite logical. Things that make sense tend to stick in a person's mind. So once the rules are understood—and understanding them isn't difficult—they probably won't be forgotten.

CHAPTER 2

DESIGNING YOUR TEST

Before you begin to write a test, think about what you want the test to accomplish. What is it, exactly, that you want to measure? Presumably you will test on the content or abilities that you most want your students to have learned. You must feel confident that the test you develop is capable of telling you what you want to know about who has learned what.

Simplicity, Simplicity, Simplicity

Anything that makes a question (or an entire test) more difficult than it needs to be affects the validity of the test. The first rule of test-making is one that every other rule supports:

Rule 1 **Make the task of taking the test as simple as possible.**

This does not mean that the test itself must be simple. It means that the examinee should know, at all times, exactly what he or she is being asked to do. It also means that the *knowing examinee* should be able to produce, or select, the correct answer with relative ease. The knowing examinee should never, ever wonder what is being asked of him or her or become confused about any part of the test. In addition, it means that the test should not involve unnecessary, repetitive, annoying, or distracting reading or actions.

Well, just think about it. What do you want to test? If it's knowledge, mastery, skill acquisition, or anything related to those things, then the task of taking the test must be very, very simple. If you break the first rule, what you will really test is the students' ability to withstand frustration or deal with confusion.

Rule 1 has to do with everything on a test—the directions you provide for a section of items, the clarity of the items themselves, the way you arrange the answers for multiple-choice items, the length of the test…everything. Every other rule is subordinate to this one because every other rule involves a way to adhere to this one.

Test Format Types

Some item formats are eschewed by writers of standardized tests because of either the items' chance factor or the complications involved in lowering their chance factor. That said, there are many formats you can choose among for a test, and you can combine any or all of them. Except for mathematics and science tests, which often contain problems and problem sets, the most common formats consist of:

- Multiple-Choice
- True/False (or a variation, such as Yes/No)
- Matching
- Fill-in-the-Blank or Completion
- Short-Answer
- Essay

Each format is suited to some kinds of content or skills and not to others. And there are benefits and drawbacks to each format. This is why many tests have two or more formats.

Multiple-Choice

Multiple-choice tests are enormously popular among test makers, for several reasons: The format is familiar, questions can be written on almost any subject, and the tests are easy to score. Multiple-choice tests are also popular among test takers for one reason: The correct answer is already on the page and usually must simply be recognized rather than formulated.

Benefits: This format adapts itself to a range of types of measurement. Of course, it can be used to test recall, but it is by no means limited to this purpose. Well-written multiple-choice items can be used to test much more complex areas of mastery, such as inference, application, analysis, and evaluation. They can be used for any question that has either one right answer or a few right answers. If items are presented with four or five answer choices, and the incorrect choices function as distractors, the chance factor is reasonably low and the validity high. And they are ideal for the type of post-test review mentioned earlier.

Drawbacks: Like all objective-test formats, the multiple-choice format is useless for determining whether the student can come up with the correct answer on his or her own or for testing interpretation. Multiple-choice items are often difficult to write well. There will be many times when writing a good stem and the correct answer choice is relatively easy, but there simply aren't three (or four) good distractors.

True/False

True/False (or Yes/No) items are also popular.

Benefits: This format can test a wide variety of skills and knowledge. Because the items can be answered quickly, they can be used to cover a great deal of material. Unlike the multiple-choice format, this format can be used when there are only two possibilities that would be attractive to an unknowing but clever examinee. (That is, the item need not present incorrect answer choices that function as distractors.) Like items in other objective formats, these items are easy to score. Even more important, they can be easy to write, although precautions must be taken, including making sure the test items do not hinge on opinion.

Drawbacks: A major disadvantage to this format is the very reason that it is scorned by standardized tests: The chance factor is 50 percent. That is, the student has a 50–50 chance of getting the right answer without having any understanding of what is being tested or without even reading the question. (Ways to reduce the chance-factor problem are described in Chapter 4.)

Matching

Matching items are, of course, an old standby and are commonly found on teacher-made tests.

Benefits: The matching format is quite useful for testing relationships (between events and dates, people and roles, words and definitions, etc.).

It can cover a great deal of information in very little space. The items are easy to write. Distractors do not have to be constructed because they are already present—as the keyed responses for other items. The chance factor, overall, is low.

Drawbacks: The format can be used to test only limited kinds of knowledge, and most of these fall within the "recall" area. It is a dangerous format to use when fine distinctions are required. The chance factor is higher than it appears to be at first glance because, on most matching sections of tests, once an answer choice is used, it is no longer a distractor for other items. Therefore, the last few items have only a few remaining answer choices. In addition, it is usually impossible for an examinee to get only one item wrong. (Ways to reduce these problems are described in Chapter 5.)

Fill-in-the-Blank

Fill-in-the-blank items eliminate the need for distractors and, perhaps for that reason, are commonly used on any test that isn't machine-scored.

Benefits: This format is useful for testing many kinds of factual information. The items are easy to write. The chance factor is often nonexistent and, even when there is a chance factor, it is usually quite low. (For example, "The first Crusade took place in the _____ century" has a chance factor because there are a limited number of centuries.) Because students must construct their own responses, this kind of item tests whether they know the answer rather than whether they are able to recognize the correct answer when it is put in front of them.

Drawbacks: The format is not very flexible; it cannot be used when the best answer is longer than one word or phrase. There are often several correct answers, so care must be taken and judgment exercised in scoring. Distinctions between "correct" and "incorrect" can be difficult to establish.

Short-Answer

Short-answer items fall into that vast area between fill-in-the-blank and essay questions. They can be several sentences long or up to two paragraphs long. Not only are they useful for several reasons, but they are sure to be involved on tests of the CCSS, so practice with them will be good for your students.

Benefits: Short-answer items have all of the benefits of fill-in-the-blank items and more. This item type is extremely flexible and can be used to test a wide range of skills from recall to analysis and evaluation. The answer requirements can range from a phrase to a paragraph or two. The format allows for more discrimination possibilities than merely "right" or "wrong." There can be "really good" answers, "decent" answers, "poor" answers, and "totally off the mark" answers.

Drawbacks: The ease of writing the questions is offset by the labor involved in scoring the answers. Many judgments must be made in the process of scoring. In addition, like essay questions, these items favor facile writers and those who can pretend to be knowledgeable, while they penalize knowledgeable students who do not express themselves well.

Essay

At grade levels between upper elementary and senior year of high school, these items are typically found at the ends of tests. College tests often consist wholly of essay items. While most of a typical elementary or high-school test (and many a college test) consists of other item types, it is often useful to round out the test with one, two, or, perhaps, a choice of essay questions.

Benefits: This is the best item type for testing higher-order thinking skills. Essay questions are unparalleled in their capacity for revealing a student's skills in analyzing, organizing, and synthesizing material. They are excellent for exploring the student's knowledge of broad issues and generalities. They are one of the two ways, along with short-answer, to test interpretation. They allow for the expression of opinions and encourage original thinking and expression. Unlike all but the very best objective test items, they do not penalize the divergent thinker.

Drawbacks: It is difficult to write essay questions that are neither too broad nor too narrow. Because of the time involved in answering them, a test cannot contain many questions, which limits the amount of material that can be covered. They are not an efficient way to test facts. They give an advantage to students who know little but say it well and those who can write quickly. They penalize those who think or write more slowly, even if their knowledge is deeper and their responses more well-reasoned. They penalize any student who writes poorly, regardless of his or her understanding of the subject matter. *And they are extremely difficult to score.* This difficulty is not just a matter of the time involved in scoring, although that is a significant issue. The scoring of essay question answers is, of necessity, subjective. As a result, any inconsistency on the part of the scorer can make the scores unreliable. Different scorers, or even the same person scoring the test a second time, may give the answer a different score.

Mixing Formats

Using several formats on the same test is fine. Doing so can often help you develop a test that measures a wider range of what you want to measure than would be possible by using only one format. Also, students vary widely in their preferences for particular formats, so using a variety tends to be fairer than using only one format. However, no matter how many formats you use, you would be well-advised to keep all the items of a particular format together. Mixing formats, such as interspersing an occasional true/false item in with multiple-choice items, causes stop/start adjustments that violate Rule 1; it simply gets in the way of efficient test-taking.

If you use several formats, you will need to decide how many points to assign to each item of a particular format. Surely you would want to give more points for a good essay question response than a correctly answered multiple-choice or true/false item. You might want to also give more points for a correctly answered multiple-choice item than a correctly answered true/false item. Give some thought to this, and weigh the item formats in a way that makes sense to you. The examinees should be told how the points will be assigned so they can spend appropriate time and effort on the various sections.

Rule 2 Use the item format most appropriate for assessing what you want to assess.

Too Easy, Too Hard?

If most examinees can get most of the items right regardless of whether they understand the material being tested, what does the test accomplish? If only a few examinees can get any of the items right regardless of whether they have the level of understanding that you expect, again, what have you accomplished? In either case, nothing.

Discrimination isn't always bad. As a matter of fact, it is the purpose of testing, which is to discriminate among levels of knowledge or skill or ability to problem-solve.

If one has to have a thorough grasp of all the material in order to answer any of the questions on a test, then the only possible grades on the test are A's and F's. Do you really want to give a flunking grade to the students who read and listened and tried? To those who sort of got it? Pretty much got it? Probably not. But if your test is too hard, this is the result you will be stuck with. On the other hand, do you want to give an A to every student who skimmed the material or stayed awake in class? Again, probably not. But this is what will result from a test that is too easy. And reviewing the test afterward will not be very productive.

Good tests have, in effect, something for everyone—that is, everyone who is at all prepared. A good test reveals who read the material or listened to your lectures or explanations and who didn't. It also reveals who sort of understood what he or she read or heard and who didn't, and who really got it and who didn't. No test can answer all these questions unless it contains items of varying difficulty and depth.

In general, it is a good idea to begin any test with items on the easier end of the scale of difficulty. Anything that positively affects a test-taker's attitude increases the validity of the test results. Those who meet with success early in a test are likely to keep working on it, while those who can't answer even the first question or two often give up immediately.

CHAPTER 3

MULTIPLE-CHOICE QUESTIONS

Unfortunately, one of the most useful of all formats—the ubiquitous multiple-choice—is the hardest to do right. The very familiarity of the format can cause serious problems. If everyone thinks there's nothing to it, the inevitable result is poor tests. And there is quite a bit to it. There is a world of difference between a good multiple-choice item and a bad one. The rules for writing good items are not difficult to follow, but you must understand what they are and why they exist. Also, of course, once you understand how to write good multiple-choice items, you will find it much easier to recognize a bad item when you see one.

Style

Let's deal first with what a multiple-choice item should look like, how it should be arranged on the page. This part is really easy. It's also important, because it affects the task of taking the test.

The Stem

A stem can take the form of a complete sentence with a question mark at the end or an incomplete statement that can be correctly completed by only one of the answer choices.

Complete stem item:

Who broke Baby Bear's chair?

A. Baby Bear

B. Mama Bear

C. Papa Bear

D. Goldilocks

Incomplete stem item:

Baby Bear's chair was broken by

A. Baby Bear.   C. Papa Bear.

B. Mama Bear.   D. Goldilocks.

Many ideas, facts, and concepts can be tested either way. Some people rant about incomplete stems, believing them to be unclear, subversive, or worse. The truth is that if the item itself is written correctly, students have no more difficulty dealing with one style than with the other.

How to Choose

Some items demand an incomplete stem on the basis of efficiency. This may occur with answer choices that repeat the same information. The information could be added to the stem. This is also helpful to the examinee. The less the examinee has to read, the more time he or she has available to think.

Inefficient item:

After the ball, how was the Prince able to locate Cinderella?

A. She had left her address.

B. She had left her glass slipper.

C. She had left a trail of breadcrumbs.

D. She had left fingerprints and DNA evidence.

Efficient item:

After the ball, the Prince was able to locate Cinderella because she had left

A. her address.

B. her glass slipper.

C. a trail of breadcrumbs.

D. fingerprints and DNA evidence.

The Answer Choices

These are the words, phrases, or sentences from which the examinee must select an answer. The more answer choices there are, the lower the chance factor. However, since it is difficult to develop good distractors, which is what incorrect answers are supposed to be, there are practical limitations on the number. The most common number is either four or five, but three is also popular.

Answer-Choice Formats

Answer choices can be arranged horizontally:

What did Goldilocks eat at the Three Bears' house?

A. honey   B. cookies   C. porridge   D. pancakes

They can be arranged vertically:

What was Goldilocks doing when the Three Bears returned home?

A. having breakfast

B. prowling around the house

C. sitting in Papa Bear's chair

D. sleeping in Baby Bear's bed

They can be arranged in two columns, as in the broken chair items shown earlier.

The length of the answer choices is the only factor you need to consider in deciding which style to use, and you can arrange the choices for one item vertically (because they're long), the next set horizontally (because they're short), and the next set in two columns (because they're in-between).

Sequencing Answer Choices

Remember Rule 1? The one about making the task of taking the test as easy as possible? This is the rule to bear in mind as you position the answer choices into an A, B, C, D, and maybe E sequence. Arrange the choices by length, from shortest to longest or the reverse, unless there is an overriding reason to arrange them another way. At best, it is annoying to have to read a long answer choice, a short one, a short one, and another long one. At worst, burying a short answer among longer ones tends to obscure it.

Poorly arranged item:

Which of the following presented the greatest danger to the settlers in Williamsburg?

A. their insistence on growing tobacco, a cash crop, instead of food crops

B. disease

C. the impossibility of adequately patrolling and protecting the frontier

D. floods

The answer, by the way, is A. (Without a Piggly Wiggly down the road, the profits these people made from selling tobacco were of little help in keeping them alive.) But which answer is correct isn't the point here; the point is that answers B and D are hard to find.

Since it really isn't any harder to arrange answer choices in order of length, why not do it? Besides, it looks better, which makes the test look more professional.

Following this recommendation will allow you to see immediately whether your tests manifest another common ailment, indicated by the "if it's long, it's right" feature. If you tend to provide more detail for the correct answer than for the distractors, you will see this flaw immediately because you will have a disproportionate number of keyed responses in the last or next to last position. Then you can fix this flaw instead of having the validity of your test fall victim to all those examinees who may not have studied but are clever enough to have seen what you were blissfully unaware you were doing.

Overriding Problems

Sometimes the answer choices for an item involve such things as time, degree, or size that dictate the sequence of the choices. If there is a natural sequence to the choices, arrange them according to that natural sequence. Failing to do so makes items irritating and confusing to read and answer.

Illogical sequence:

How many deciduous teeth (baby teeth) does a child have?

A. 28   B. 16   C. 20   D. 32

Logical sequence:

How many deciduous teeth (baby teeth) does a child have?

A. 16   B. 20   C. 28   D. 32

Illogical sequence:

When did Rufus Slaphappy leave on his walk?

A. right after lunch

B. right before lunch

C. right before dinner

D. as breakfast was served

Logical sequence:

A. as breakfast was served

B. right before lunch

C. right after lunch

D. right before dinner

Content

OK, so now you know what a multiple-choice item should look like. Now let's deal with what is should *be* like.

Keyed Response vs. Right Answer(s)

Rule 3 **When the directions say to select one answer, provide one and only one correct answer among the choices.**

The reasoning behind this rule is simple. If there is not a correct answer, the question is worthless. If there is more than one correct answer, the same holds true because a student can select a correct answer without getting credit for doing so. So why am I even mentioning it? Because failure to obey it is common. No one ever means to disobey it, but test-writers do so with chilling regularity. The answer key may identify a keyed response, but the question may actually have no right answer or several right answers. This problem appears on every kind of test imaginable. It shouldn't appear anywhere.

No right answer:

Which word is spelled wrong?

A. cote

C. trot

B. lion

D. blue

None of these words is spelled wrong. Granted, a student who might wonder about the spelling of *lion, trot,* and *blue* is unlikely to know that *cote* is a correctly spelled word.

No matter. It is. It is the wrong way to spell *coat,* but it is the right way to spell the name of a cooplike structure.

More than one right answer:

Which of the following has five sides?

A. triangle   C. pentagon

B. hexagon   D. parallelogram

There are two correct answers. A hexagon has one side in addition to five, but a hexagon does have five sides. ("Do you have a dollar?" can be answered in the affirmative whether you have one dollar or ten thousand.)

More than one right answer:

What kind of poem is Rossetti's "Nuptial Sleep"?

A. ode

B. lyric

C. ballad

D. sonnet

Again, there are two right answers. Since all sonnets are lyric poetry, both B and D are correct.

Focusing the Stem

Rule 4 Write the stem of a multiple-choice item in such a way that the knowing examinee could write the desired answer on a blank line following it.

A good multiple-choice item presents the central problem in the stem, thereby focusing the examinee's mental processes. If you follow Rule 4, *this will always occur.* Following this rule will do more to improve your multiple-choice items than any other single change in the way you do things.

To understand the point of the rule, think about why multiple-choice items exist. Let's say you want to know whether your students know why Romeo committed suicide. Why not just ask them? "Why did Romeo commit suicide?" Well, then you'd have to read all those answers. You'd have to decide whether "His heart was broken" or "He didn't want to live without Juliet" counts as an adequately complete answer. You'd have to spend longer scoring the test than you'd spent writing it. It's easier, fairer, and far more efficient to limit the examinee's possible responses, and once you've done that, you have a multiple-choice item.

Multiple-choice items exist because they are easier to score than open-ended questions. The answer choices are present on the page to simplify the scoring process. A knowing examinee, having read the stem, should be able to skim the answer choices to locate the one that comes closest to expressing the same fact or concept that he or she has already mentally determined is the answer.

Let's try it. Here's a good stem:

> The Three Bears were not at home when Goldilocks arrived because they...

Quickly now, what's the answer? It's something like "had gone for a walk." Given a set of answer choices, you would skim right over such choices as "had moved to Toledo" and "were in the emergency room with stomach cramps" while looking for something having to do with going for a walk.

Here's a bad stem:

> When Goldilocks arrived at the Three Bears' house, they… Quickly now, what's the answer? "Huh?" you say? And well you might. Is it "Had left the door unlocked" or "weren't at home" or "had left their breakfast on the table" or…?

A stem like this should be put to bed without any porridge at all. It requires the examinee to read and judge every answer choice to see if it completes a true statement about the story. That's a waste of time and, worse, requires non-productive thought. An item that can be correctly answered only by eliminating wrong answers is a flawed item.

The Exception to the Rule

All right, it's true, sometimes you have to write a stem that fails to present the central problem. You just have to. All "Which of the following…?" items are examples. This is because students won't know which choice is the correct answer until they read all of the choices. You don't have to purge every last one of such items from your tests. What you do have to do is to narrow the scope of inquiry as much as possible and then focus it with your first answer choice, which is not necessarily the correct answer. All remaining answer choices must follow in parallel fashion, both grammatically and conceptually. The examinee who doesn't know what you were getting at with the stem *will* know as soon as he or she reads the first answer choice.

Parallel choices:

Jerome threw the pie at

A. a stranger.

B. the babysitter.

C. his brother Charlie.

D. his cousin Ferdinand.

As soon as the examinee sees "a stranger," he or she knows that the question deals with a "whom."

Nonparallel choices:

Jerome threw the pie at

A. four o'clock.

B. the babysitter.

C. hearing bad news.

D. a critical moment in his life.

A Final Word on This Subject

A multiple-choice item that does not focus on the scope of inquiry is really a set of true/false items dressed up to look like one multiple-choice item. If what you really want to do is to write a true/false test, do so in a true/false format. Don't write a set of true/false items (only one of which is true or only one of which is false) that masquerades as a multiple-choice item. If it walks like a set of true/false items and it quacks like a set of true/false items, it's a set of true/false items. Here is an example. Only A is a true statement. The rest are false statements about the poem.

Flawed item:

In Wordsworth's "Composed Upon Westminster Bridge,"

A. the place setting is urban.

B. the time setting is evening.

C. the mood is one of excitement.

D. the speaker is unfamiliar with the bridge.

Focusing the Answer Choices

Rule 5 **Include no answer choice that includes any other answer choice.**

This problem often occurs when details are being tested. It's easier to show than to explain.

What is the *Venus de Milo* missing?

A. feet   C. arms

B. legs   D. head

This particular example does not create a problem for the knowing examinee because C, and only C, is the correct answer. However, it creates a problem for the test maker by effectively reducing the number of actual answer choices from four to three. Answer B cannot be correct. If it were, answer A would also have to be correct. So there are really only three possible choices.

Another example is a modified version of one found on a real statewide test.

From what point of view is the passage narrated?

A. first person, Ralph   C. third person, Alice

B. third person, limited   D. third person, omniscient

Did no one notice that if C is true, B must also be true, thereby eliminating B and C as possible answers?

Distracting the Unknowing Examinee

Rule 6 **Incorrect answer choices should function as distractors. They should appeal to examinees who do not have the knowledge or skill that the item requires.**

Being able to write a good stem and a correct answer is necessary, but it is not sufficient. You must also be able to develop incorrect answer choices that serve the function of appealing to the examinee who doesn't know the answer. If such answer choices are not present, you might as well just leave the wrong-answer areas blank. If students can choose the keyed answer regardless of whether they have read or learned the material being tested, the item is flawed.

There are many, many questions that simply cannot be asked in a multiple-choice format because there are wrong answers galore but an insufficient number of distractors.

Flawed items:

Lafayette fought in the Revolutionary War on the side of the

A. British.   C. Dutch.

B. Spanish.   D. Americans.

When there are only two possible answers (in this example there were only two sides in the war), there cannot be four answer choices. The other two choices simply are not distractors.

Rover is Lydia's

A. dog.   C. brother.

B. bird.   D. Model T Ford.

This is a *much* better item if *dog* is not the answer than if it is. If the answer is A, the item is a no-brainer. The flaw is, of course, rarely this obvious, but it is extremely common. It is found with great frequency on statewide tests and even, from time to time, on nationally normed tests.

If nationally normed tests, which go through *years* of development by extremely skilled and knowledgeable authors and editors, contain this problem, you can bet that tests written the night before they will be given do too. An item with too few wrong answers that function as distractors can sometimes be turned into a reasonable true/false or short-answer item:

On which side did Lafayette fight in the Revolutionary War? _____

Other Issues

Keeping Items Discrete

Rule 7 **All items must be discrete, that is, independent of each other.**

This rule means that the stem of one item should not give away the answer to another item. It also means that the same fact should not be tested twice. It should always be possible to get one item wrong without necessarily getting another one wrong too. It should always be possible to get one item right without necessarily getting another one right too.

Flawed items:

Why are the people of Hammond worried?

A. Too many people are moving there.

B. Their farms are not producing enough.

C Gangs have started to form in the town.

D. The nearby city is growing and moving too close.

What is the main threat to Hammond?

A. an uncertain climate

B. economic uncertainty

C. air and water pollution

D. violence from gang activity

Would it be possible to answer the first question correctly (C) without also answering the second correctly (D)? Would it be possible to get one of them right and the other wrong? These two items, no matter how distant they are from each other physically, are covering precisely the same point.

Signaling the Keyed Response

You can ask a perfectly good, clearly worded, appropriately difficult question and then ruin its effectiveness by unconsciously supplying signals for what the correct answer is. Students are extremely good at recognizing such signals. Some of the most common are:

A. providing more detail for the keyed response than for other choices. The keyed response should be as brief as possible; distractors should not significantly differ in length from the keyed response.

B. including absolutes ("only," "ever," etc.) only for distractors or including qualifiers ("often," "usually," "relatively," etc.) only for the keyed response. Students are well aware that it is often difficult to be definitive in writing a correct answer.

C. including wrong choices that do not "fit" the stem grammatically. If an incomplete stem ends with *a*, no answer choice that begins with a vowel sound could be correct. Of course, the reverse holds true for stems that end with *an*.

D. positioning the keyed response too frequently in the same place. For some reason, many test-writers suffer from either the A syndrome or the C syndrome, placing more keyed responses in either the first or third position. These are mysterious syndromes, perhaps having to do with a dominant gene. Your students will rapidly figure out whether you suffer from either one. In the finished test the keyed answer should appear about an equal number of times in each answer position.

Negative Stems

Negative stems have a bad reputation. They are those stems that use the dreaded *not* word, as in "Which of the following is not the name of one of the Seven Dwarfs?" So what's wrong with that? Not much but enough: The *not* is in hiding.

The real issue is, of course, clarity. Will a student who reads the stem quickly realize that he or she should be looking for an exception? If the stem uses *not*, and it is buried among other words, it may be missed. So, don't bury it. Capitalize it, or boldface it, or make it obvious in some other way. If possible, position it near the end of the stem.

Many teachers believe that *not* items are confusing. They don't have to be confusing, and there are times when they work better than any other type of wording to get at what you want to know. Sometimes using "except" can make an item clearer, as in "All of the following are names of the Seven Dwarfs EXCEPT…"

A cautionary note: never, ever, *ever* follow a negatively worded stem with any answer choice that also includes a negative. Doing so sets up mental hurdles that are difficult to leap in order to get at what is being asked.

So, it's time to repeat Rule 1: Make the task of taking the test as easy as possible. If a negatively stated stem breaks that rule, rewrite it until it doesn't.

CHAPTER 4

TRUE/FALSE QUESTIONS

True/false questions (or yes/no or any "alternate response" format) are scorned by publishers of standardized tests. This is due to their very high chance factor. Because the chance factor is 50 percent, the lowest score that a completely unknowing examinee could be expected to get is also 50 percent. This means that there isn't much room left to discriminate among poor, average, good, and exceptional mastery or knowledge. The format, however, retains its popularity in more casual testing situations because it can be used to test a wide variety of types of material and because the questions are so easy to write. And there is nothing wrong with using alternate-response items if you include enough of them to counteract the effects of the chance factor.

Format Variations

The basic alternate-response format can be presented in several ways. The most common are:

Directions: On the blank line, write *T* if the statement is true and *F* if it is false.

_____The state with the most income from farming is Iowa.

Directions: Circle *T* if the statement is true and *F* if it is false.

The longest chain of mountains above sea level is the Andes.

T   F

Directions: Circle the correct answer for each question.

Did Harriet Beecher Stowe write *Uncle Tom's Cabin*?

Yes   No

It is also possible to explore a particular body of knowledge by presenting an incomplete statement that can be completed in a variety of ways, each of which must be judged to be either true or false:

In order for airplane wings to produce lift, there must be

A. greater air pressure on the lower surface than on the upper.   T   F

B. a slower flow of air along the upper surface than the lower.   T   F

C. an angle between the wings and airflow equal to   T   F
   or more than 20 degrees.

All of these forms are useful if they are constructed correctly. None of them is useful if it is not. The fact that they are easy to write does not mean that there are no rules. Of course there are rules!

Content

Rule 8 **Keep your language simple and clear.**

Anything that interferes with the examinee's ability to understand what is being asked negatively affects the validity of the item. Shun ambiguous terms, such as *several* or *frequently*, which mean different things to different people, and words the express value, such as *worst*. Use the most precise language you can use. "One in 30 people" is clear, whereas "few" is ambiguous; "cleanest-burning" is inarguable whereas "best" is a matter of opinion. And never present a negative statement in a true/false format. Asking examinees to judge whether a negative statement is false requires them to deal with a double negative.

Thomas Jefferson was NOT the third president of the United States.

Rule 9 **Construct alternate-response items so that it is clear what you are asking about or getting at.**

Do not present statements that are substantially true with one false detail.

Tricky item:

When Columbus set sail from Italy in 1492, he intended to reach the East by sailing west.

Straightforward items:

Columbus' first voyage of discovery began in 1492.
On his voyages of discovery, Columbus set sail from Italy.
On Columbus' first voyage of discovery, he intended to reach the East by sailing west.

All information *except the part being questioned* must be accurate. Do not sneak an untrue detail into a true statement to trip up the unwary. All that is indicated by an examinee's failure to get such an item right is that he or she should not plan on a career as a proofreader.

Rule 10 **Signal the concept being questioned.**

This is just as important in alternate-response items as it is in multiple-choice items. Construct all alternate-response questions so that it is completely clear what fact is in question.

Unfocused item:

Gregor Mendel, an Austrian monk, used garden peas to study inherited traits.

What is actually being asked? Was it Mendel who did this? Was he a monk? Did he live in Austria? Was he studying inherited traits? Did he use garden peas in his studies or, perhaps, cauliflower? The entire statement is true, but the item is still seriously flawed because five questions had to be answered to determine that.

Focused items:

The person who formulated the first correct theory of heredity was Gregor Mendel.

The plants used by Mendel to study inherited traits were garden peas.

The plant traits that Mendel studied were those that are inherited.

Writing reasonable, fair, and valid true/false questions is not a difficult task. All one need do is decide what one fact to test and then make the statement signal the concept in question. Violating either of these construction rules results in what are, in effect, trick questions. Leave those to game show hosts; they do not belong on any serious test.

Other Issues

Unintentional Clues

As is the case with multiple-choice items, it is a truly rare student who, by about the sixth grade, has not figured out that statements that include *all, none, always,* or *never* tend to be false while those that include *many, often, frequently,* or *some* tend to be true. Therefore, it is better to avoid statements that, in order to be clearly true or clearly false, must contain such qualifiers. The complete set of true-false items should have about an equal number of true statements and false statements. (The examinee should not be able to get a good score by marking every statement false or every statement true.)

Reducing the Chance Factor

The desire to reduce the chance factor on true/false items has led to a potentially useful, but often sloppily executed, complication. Examinees may be asked to revise any false statements to make them true. This is a nice idea in theory, and it can work just swell if it's developed properly. Unfortunately, one often sees statements such as the following.

Unfocused variation:

Directions: If the statement is true, write *true* on the blank line. If it is false, rewrite the statement to make it true.

Rusting is an example of a physical change in a substance.

_____

Did you say, "What's wrong with that?" I'll pretend you did, because I'm longing to tell you. The statement is problematic because, although it is clearly false, the examinee can correct it in any number of perfectly adequate ways:

1. Evaporation is an example of a physical change in a substance.

2. Melting is an example of a physical change in a substance.

3. Condensation is an example of a physical change in a substance.

4. Rusting is an example of what happens to cars in Chicago.

5. Rusting is an example of a chemical change in a substance.

6. Rusting is not an example of a physical change in a substance.

An unfocused false statement to be corrected confuses the examinee, who doesn't necessarily know how you want the statement fixed, and causes untold headaches for you in grading the test. Give the examinee and yourself a break. Rewrite the instruction line. Then target something!

Focused variation:

Directions: If the statement is true, write *true* on the blank line. If it is false, replace the underlined word or phrase with a word or phrase that makes the statement true.

Rusting is an example of a <u>physical change</u> in a substance.

_____

Now only answer 5 is correct. The knowing examinee will know immediately to write "chemical change" on the blank line. The unknowing examinee will write something else. Much neater, much tidier, much easier to score, and *much* more informative about whether the students know what you hope they know.

CHAPTER 5

MATCHING QUESTIONS

When the matching format works, it's a peach. It's an ideal way to test whos, whats, and wheres when there are enough similar bits of information to be tested this way. Examinees can be asked to match, for example, inventors with inventions, words with definitions, substances with melting points, or presidents with legislation. However, if you want to test both inventors and melting points, don't try to do this in the same matching section.

Design Considerations

Practicality sets limits on the length of any matching section on a test. Because this format requires the examinee to repeatedly look through the answer choices to identify the letter of the correct answer, even if he or she knows what the answer is, the number of options must be limited. More than 15 choices can create both confusion and frustration, but presenting fewer than five simply doesn't provide enough options.

The entire matching section must appear on the same page. It is confusing and burdensome to require an examinee to go back and forth from one page to another to find the correct response to an item.

If logic can be imposed on the arrangement of answer choices, impose it. Response options that can be arranged alphabetically, numerically, or chronologically should be arranged in such a fashion because doing so will allow the knowing examinee to quickly locate the answer he or she is looking for. If there is no logic to impose, at least be careful not to bury short answer possibilities among longer ones.

Content

Rule 11 Construct homogeneous lists for matching items.

Matching items should test knowledge, not basic logic skills. When different types of names, terms, or concepts are provided for matching purposes, the examinee can often either eliminate inappropriate response options or choose the only plausible response.

Motley crew items:

_____ quota system	A. a method of limiting immigration
_____ Five-Power Treaty	B. Warren G. Harding's secretary of state
_____ Sacco and Vanzetti	C. an illegal use of public oil reserves for private gain
_____ Teapot Dome Scandal	D. an arms control agreement limiting warships
_____ Charles Evans Hughes	E. anarchists convicted, on weak evidence, of armed robbery

The problem with the above example is, of course, that there are no distractors. Each term on the left can be logically matched with only one answer.

Homogeneous items:

_____ John L. Lewis

_____ Mitchell Palmer

_____ Andrew Mellon

_____ Albert B. Fall

_____ Charles Evans Hughes

A. a banker, financier, philanthropist, and secretary of the treasury

B. secretary of the Interior involved in the Teapot Dome Scandal

C. labor leader who strengthened the United Mine Workers Union

D. secretary of state who became chief justice of the United States

E. Attorney general who trampled civil rights in a search for anarchists, socialists, and communists

In addition to eliminating simple logic as the tested skill, homogenous items provide distractors aplenty as long as the relative difficulty of the individual items is roughly similar. If it is not, the number of answer choices that function as distractors plummets.

Items of uneven difficulty:

_____ sirenia

_____ monotreme

_____ predator

_____ ungulate

_____ vertebrate

A. a hoofed mammal

B. a mammal that lays eggs

C. an animal with a backbone

D. an animal that hunts live prey

E. a large, vegetarian sea mammal

Because both *predator* and *vertebrate* are familiar vocabulary to many people, even those who have not studied zoology, this matching set consists in *effect* of only three items.

Examining Answer Choices

Although there can be more answer choices than there are items, there simply cannot be multiple correct responses. This is a common problem, probably because those correct, but unintended, matches can sneak up on the test writer in certain situations. When you construct a set of matching items, *you must pay close attention to all of the answer choices you are providing.* You cannot, as with multiple-choice items, provide wrong answers specifically designed to be distractors for your question if they could be thought to have another reason for being there.

Multiple correct answers:

Directions: Match each item on the left with its synonym on the right.

_____ 1. eclipse	A. conceal
_____ 2. simulate	B. construct
_____ 3. manipulate	C. exceed
_____ 4. fabricate	D. handle
_____ 5. obscure	E. pretend

Item 1 can be correctly matched with either A or C, and item 4 can be correctly matched with B or E.

Other Issues

Directions

It is absolutely critical that directions (an instruction line) spell out the basis for the matching and make it clear whether an answer choice may, or may not, be used more than once.

Reducing the Chance Factor

The matching format appears to have a lower chance factor than it actually has. If each answer choice is used one time, and no choice is used more than once, the list of possible choices decreases by one each time an answer is chosen. Each piece of tested knowledge possessed by the examinee provides a correct answer and reduces the distractors for remaining items.

One good way to reduce the chance factor is to provide more answer choices than items. This works when matching such facts as countries and their capitals or chemical elements and their symbols. For example:

Directions: On the blank in front of each symbol, write the letter of the chemical element that symbol represents.

_____ 1. Ag	A. Cadmium
_____ 2. C	B. Carbon
_____ 3. Sn	C. Gold
_____ 4. Au	D. Iron
_____ 5. Fe	E. Lead
_____ 6. Hg	F. Mercury
	G. Potassium
	H. Silver
	I. Sodium
	J. Tin

Note that the answer choices are arranged alphabetically. This makes it easy for the student who knows the chemical element denoted by the symbol to find it, and its answer-choice letter, quickly.

Reducing the chance factor also assists in correcting a related problem that exists in the one-to-one matching format, which is that it is impossible to get only one item wrong.

CHAPTER 6

COMMON MISTAKES ON SELECTED-RESPONSE TESTS

The ideal test of any type discriminates between the knowing and the unknowing examinee. It is clear in what it asks examinees to do. It provides you with useful information about your students. It tests only knowledge and skills that can be tested with the format chosen. The selected-response test cannot be used to test interpretation. It uses only objective questions. "Objective questions" are those for which one, and only one, answer has been predetermined to be correct. All multiple-choice, matching, and true/false items are "objective questions." Most fill-in-the-blank ones are too, as are most short-answer questions, although these may allow for variations in wording. Attempts to test interpretation, for which a wide variety of answers may well be considered correct, with an objective question are neither productive nor fair.

All questions should be worded so that students understand what is being asked of them. If you do not know for a fact that your students know the meaning of *unique* (and it is a rare student below 9th grade who does), you cannot use this word in a test question regardless of how badly you want to, unless what you mean to test is whether your students know the word.

Even if you use selected-response items to test the right kind of things, there are some common mistakes that test writers make. Avoiding them will greatly improve your tests.

Common Mistakes

Here are some mistakes that test writers often make when writing selected-response tests. Getting them out of your system—and your tests—will make you a much better test writer.

Asking Questions with More than One Correct Answer

The tendency to direct students to choose "the best answer" does not relieve any item writer of the responsibility for constructing an answer that is clearly correct. This means that a test developer must avoid all answer choices that are almost correct or that could be considered correct by the divergent thinker. Distractors are meant to distract only the unknowing examinee, never the knowing examinee.

Any question that does not have a correct answer and only one correct answer that is clearly stated does not belong on a selected-response test.

Not Getting to the Heart of the Matter

Test items should always go directly to the heart of the matter. This is especially true of multiple-choice items. Think about what it is you want to know. Then ask *that* question.

Flawed item:

A test on the story "Seventh Grade" by Gary Soto asked the following question:

What kind of face does Michael think it is cool to make?

A. a frown

B. a big smile

C. a funny face

D. a scowl

Answer choices A and D are not discrete. A scowl is a type of frown. Answer choice C can be defended since Michael's friend Victor describes the kind of face as a "funny face."

Advice for fix: What's important? In this case, what's important is that Michael very much wants to be cool. Don't present the important issue in the stem; ask about it! Keep answer choices discrete.

Valid item:

Why does Michael scowl?

A. to look cool

B. to impress Victor

C. to frighten people

D. to express his feelings

Testing the Wrong Thing

If, for example, you are testing acquired vocabulary, do not provide context clues. If you are testing context clues, be sure the target word is unfamiliar to most examinees.

Flawed item:

The following item was intended to test vocabulary acquisition, not the ability to use context clues:

No one expected the ship to <u>collide</u> with an iceberg.

A. steer

B. freeze

C. crash

D. sail

Assuming that the fifth graders who were to be tested know *iceberg* (and if they don't, there's another, bigger flaw in the item), is it possible that anyone could describe a situation in which anything but choice C is conceivable?

Advice for fix: Always use a minimum of other words and no context clues at all in a vocabulary acquisition item.

Valid item:

No one expected the canoes to <u>collide</u>.

A. race

B. sink

C. crash

D. tip over

Anything that gets in the way of testing what you mean to test can be called a "contaminant." The most common contaminant is readability. Unless difficult vocabulary is what you mean to test, it has no place on a test. The following examples exaggerate the problem to make it clear. However, just because items flawed in this way are usually more subtle does not mean that this is not a huge and common problem.

Flawed items:

Joe has 3 apples, 9 pears, and 15 bananas. What is the aggregate number of pieces of fruit that Joe has?

A. 3

B. 9

C. 15

D. 27

Does *aggregate* mean "fewest," "average," "greatest," or "total"?

To vex means to

A. pique.

B. flatter.

C. coerce.

D. frighten.

Even the student who knows perfectly well what *vex* means is unlikely to know that *pique* is a synonym.

Another common contaminant in vocabulary items is the use of more than one part of speech in the answer choices. This not only makes it harder for the student to read and think about the item, but it also may eliminate some answer choices by lack of grammatical fit with the stem.

Not Using Distractors

The incorrect answer choices must function as distractors. If no half-awake examinee would, under any circumstances, ever choose a particular response, it is not a distractor. Non-distractors include those choices that seem to come "from left field." That is, they have nothing to do with the passage and would be rejected by anyone even faintly familiar with it.

Flawed item:

The following item was part of a test on the poem "Knoxville," by Nikki Giovanni:

The speaker says she enjoys summer because she can be warm all the time, not only when going to bed and sleeping. This implies that

A. a warm bed is only comfortable in summer.

B. she likes winter more than summer.

C. her family had no heat during the winter.

D. she does not like to sleep.

This item has no distractors at all. It also doesn't have a correct answer, but the *keyed* response can be determined by eliminating the answer choices that could not possibly, in any poem or other selection, be correct. Choice A is ridiculous; it contradicts itself. Choice B is contradicted by information provided by the item writer ("enjoys"). Choice D makes no sense.

Advice for fix: There's nothing wrong with testing inference as long as something is clearly suggested, which is done by the stem. Think about what is suggested. Provide a reasonable inference as the keyed response. Provide distractors, not ridiculous and nonsensical wrong answer choices.

Valid item:

The lines about being warm all the time, not only when going to bed and sleeping, suggest that the speaker

A. is too warm all the time.

B. is often cold during other seasons.

C. sleeps too much during the summer.

D. doesn't sleep enough during other seasons.

Testing Minutiae

Never test minutiae. If some fine point or subtle distinction is worth testing, it is not minutia. If any reasonable person's response to a statement reflecting the item and its keyed response would be "So what?" it is minutia.

Passage or Knowledge-Independent Items

When comprehending a reading passage or possessing specific knowledge is supposedly needed, the items should not be answerable without the student's reading the passage or being in possession of that knowledge.

Flawed item:

Amphibians are a class of animals that can breathe in and out of water. Which of the following is an amphibian?

A. a trout

B. a gecko

C. a salamander

D. an ostrich

Most students realize that a trout is a fish (and, therefore, cannot breathe out of water) and an ostrich is a bird (and, therefore, cannot breathe in water). Those widely known facts eliminate choices A and D and give this item a 50 percent chance factor.

The following item is even worse. Common sense provides the answer, whether the student has acquired any information or not.

Flawed item:

All of the following were involved in Project Peru Amazon Adventure 2005 *except*

A. the four Americans who went.

B. 12,000 students from 100 schools.

C. two Peruvian guides.

D. all of the schools in the United States.

You've most probably never so much as heard of "Project Peru Amazon Adventure 2005," but that doesn't mean you can't leap directly to answer choice D as the keyed response. There is no way to "fix" such items. Eliminate them.

Using Incorrect Terminology

In short, do not trust any test containing items that indicate that the test writer did not, himself or herself, understand the skill being tested.

Flawed item:

The author's tone in this poem is

A. depressing.

B. playful.

C. irritated.

D. furious.

Besides the fact that one is not the "author" of a poem, since *tone* is the attitude of the speaker, narrator, or writer toward the subject, it cannot be "depressing." It would have to be "depressed." To test tone, one must use only words that could conceivably describe a tone.

Testing More than One Skill or Fact at a Time

Leave all multipart questions, including any that require defense or explanation, in the realm of the constructed-response test. They do not belong in a selected-response format.

Flawed item:

Based on the theme of the poem, you can infer that

A. the author lives with her grandmother.

B. the author wants to live anywhere but Knoxville.

C. the author enjoys Knoxville in the summer.

D. the author enjoys swimming and surfing.

There are other flaws in this item as well, but it appears that the examinee has to both identify the poem's theme and make an inference based on it. Don't make the examinee do this.

Presenting or Suggesting Falsities in the Stem

The stem of an item must never suggest, by the content or manner of wording, an untruth. The following item was intended to assess the students' ability to recognize and use certain noun-forming suffixes, in this case -*ation*.

Flawed item:

The selection says, "Even though that sounds like a lot of islands, many of them are too small for habitation." What does the word *habitation* mean?

A. not living

B. one who lives

C. living again

D. the act of living

In the lesson, suffixes are attached only to base words. However, in this item, the suffix -*ation* has not been affixed to a base word. Instead, it has been attached to a Latin root (from *habitare*), which has no connection, in a student's mind, with the base word *habit*. Therefore, this stem implies—by consideration of what examinees have been taught—that -*ation* has turned *habit* (which is already a noun) into a noun. Given the situation, this makes the stem state a falsity.

Advice for fix: Use a different word! Find a base word that is familiar. Attach to it one of the noun-forming suffixes you have been teaching to get a word that is unfamiliar (such as *furtherance*) and have at it.

Determine Whether a Test Was Valid

One quick way to tell whether a test you have administered was, indeed, a valid one is to do your own version of data collection. There is a statistic called the "point bi-serial" that is used by measurement people all over the world to analyze test items. It is a measurement involving how well an examinee who correctly answered a specific item did on the test as a whole. An item with a high point bi-serial is one that is in line with logic: Students who answered it correctly did well on the test as a whole. An item with a low point bi-serial is just the opposite. Students who answered it correctly did poorly on the test as a whole. This is a tremendously meaningful statistic because items with low point bi-serials are discriminating *against* the knowing examinee. Such items are almost inevitably severely flawed, often in a way that the test developer never imagined. One (or more) of the distractors was more attractive to the knowing examinee than the keyed response. It was more appealing for a reason, which may be that it was actually a better answer than the keyed response.

It will take only a few minutes of your time to check to see whether your most able students, those you can usually count on to listen in class, study and understand the material, and do their homework, did significantly better on the test you just gave them than your least able students. You can even go so far as to check individual items. Did the students who did well on the test as a whole do poorly in any significant way on any item or items? If they did, look hard at those items. The chances are much higher that the items are flawed than that your most able students suddenly became unknowing examinees.

If you find that one of your items is flawed, you will need to decide what to do about the situation. You could eliminate the item from the test and recalculate the scores, but this runs the risk of infuriating those students who got it right. You could decide not to count it as part of the score for those students who got it wrong and recalculate the scores of those students. Or you could leave it alone and try to figure out why this happened, resolving to be more careful next time. Whatever you decide to do, you will have learned something about how you write tests.

CHAPTER 7

FILL-IN-THE-BLANK AND COMPLETION QUESTIONS

Any incomplete-stem, multiple-choice question that has a single word or phrase answer can be presented, instead, as a fill-in-the-blank or completion item.

The cotton gin was invented by

A. Elias Howe.

C. Eli Whitney.

B. Isaac Singer.

D. Cyrus McCormick.

versus:

The cotton gin was invented by _____.

Any complete-stem, multiple-choice question that has a single word or phrase answer can be presented, instead, with a blank line following the question.

What is the outermost layer of the earth's atmosphere called?

A. mesosphere

C. thermosphere

B. stratosphere

D. troposphere

versus:

What is the outermost layer of the Earth's atmosphere called?

_____

Asking the examinee to finish an incomplete statement or to provide an answer on a blank line has a clear advantage over multiple-choice: The chance factor is, at least on the surface, zero. You do, however, have to read and judge the answers rather than merely noting whether the correct answer choice has been selected. You also have to have enough items that work in this format to justify a test section consisting of them.

Style

In any fill-in-the-blank item, the information that the item provides—information that clarifies precisely what is being asked—should appear before the blank. The blank need not end the sentence, and there may be times when it must appear early in the sentence, but every effort should be made to provide sufficient information before the blank to allow the examinee to mentally formulate the answer as the blank is reached.

Backward item:

_____ is the only metal that is liquid at room temperature.

Clear item:

The only metal that is liquid at room temperature is _____ .

Once in a while, one sees fill-in-the-blank combined with multiple-choice. Such a hybrid looks like this:

Cinderella's fairy godmother turned a _____ into a coach.

A. pear   C. pumpkin

B. tomato   D. watermelon

This sort of item usually exists only because the test writer actually wants to write a classic multiple-choice item but has difficulty constructing either a complete-sentence stem or an incomplete stem. There's nothing really *wrong* with it, and it does eliminate the problem of having to read the examinee's handwriting, but that is about the only advantage. And it can't be combined with traditional multiple-choice items in a multiple-choice section of a test because it requires a different instruction line.

Content

Constructing Fill-in-the-Blank and Completion Items

Constructing reasonable, fair, and valid items of this type is largely a matter of common sense. First and foremost, such an item must raise no doubts about what piece of information is being asked for. Merely modify Rule 4 like this: "Write the stem in such a way that the knowing examinee could write the desired answer on a blank line following it." In this format, you actually have that blank line, either following the question or embedded in it. This makes it all the more important to make it unmistakably clear to the examinee what he or she is supposed to put on it.

Rule 12 **Construct fill-in-the-blank and completion items so that they have only one correct answer.**

Unclear item:

Andorra is located in _____.

Is the answer "Europe"? Is it "between France and Spain"? Is it "the Pyrenees mountains"? All of these answers are correct. Which one did you mean to elicit?

Clear items:

Andorra is located on the continent of _____.

The country of Andorra lies between the countries of _____ and _____.

In what mountain chain is Andorra located? _____

Rule 13 **In fill-in-the-blank items, omit only significant words from the statement.**

When constructing a fill-in-the-blank item, the information to be supplied by the examinee must be important. If what is left out, to be supplied by the examinee, is unimportant, what the item ends up measuring will also be unimportant.

Insignificant omissions:

The ancient Sumerians developed a form of writing called cuneiform in which wedge-shaped symbols were pressed into _____ tablets.

Significant omissions:

Cuneiform, a form of writing in which wedge-shaped symbols were pressed into clay tablets, was originally developed by the ancient _____ .

The form of writing that was developed by the ancient Sumerians, in which wedge-shaped symbols were pressed into clay tablets, is called _____ .

A fill-in-the-blank item can contain more than one blank as long as enough information is present to keep the resulting statement from being so mutilated that clarity is lost.

Mutilated item:

In the process called _____ , green plants take in _____ and give off _____ .

Clear items:

In the process called photosynthesis, green plants take in _____ and give off _____ .

The process in which green plants take in _____ and give off oxygen is called _____ .

Other Issues

There are two common ways in which test writers provide unintentional clues for what should be written on the blank lines in these kinds of items. One is to precede the blank with the article *a* or *an*, which tells the examinee whether the missing word or phrase begins with a consonant or a vowel. The other is to vary the length of the blanks, depending on the length of the missing word or phrase.

Grammatically clued item:

A solution that prevents infection by killing bacteria is called an

_____ .

Length-clued item:

The two classes of animals that are warm-blooded are _____ and

_____ .

Both of these problems are easy to avoid. If the clearest statement necessitates preceding the blank with *a* or *an*, go with the classic "a(n)," and do it every time this situation occurs. Of course, if your students haven't seen the "a(n)" method used before, you will need to introduce them to it. As for the length of the blanks, just make them all the same length. Settle on a length that will allow for the longest missing word or phrase and make every blank this same length.

CHAPTER 8

FREE-RESPONSE (SHORT-ANSWER) QUESTIONS

Any item that leaves the examinee free to construct his or her own response is, of course, a "free-response" item, but I am using the term more narrowly. Here, "free-response" does not include items that require deep thought, analysis, significant support, or any of the things typically required in "essay" items. It refers to only those questions that can be answered in two short paragraphs or less. (Some people call these items "short-answer items.")

Free-response items:

What was Jonathan Swift's real motive in writing "A Modest Proposal"?

Name and define the three groups into which mammals can be divided, based on the development of young from fertilized eggs, and give one example of each.

Why are Charlie's races with Algernon so important to his doctors?

The second of these examples requires the longest response, but it is merely a factual recall item. Each of the others can be answered in one sentence even though they test skills significantly higher on Bloom's Taxonomy.

Style

Students assume that, if they are given a lot of space for an answer, a long answer is expected; if they are given a small amount of space, a short answer is expected. Therefore, if students are to provide answers on a printed test paper, do not provide significantly more room than is required for the ideal answer, as written in typical handwriting. Space limitations on a test paper have two benefits. They imply the length expected for the answers, and they force specificity.

Content

Compared with essay questions, free-response items allow for testing a far greater range of topics. They are easier to write than essay questions and much easier to score. Each one requires far less of an examinee's time, so more of them can be included on a test.

If you don't have time to construct a good multiple-choice test, but you either won't have time to score the answers to essay questions or such questions are not really appropriate for the material you are testing, you may choose to ask free-response items.

Free-response items can be written on any subject. They are, after all, the same questions you would ask during a conversation with a student in which you hoped to determine whether he or she knew the material. Care must be taken, nonetheless, in constructing such items.

Free-response items lose their benefits when the questions ask too much.

Inappropriately complex items:

Does Jonathan Swift succeed in making his point in "A Modest Proposal"? Why, or why not?

What are the benefits and drawbacks of group life for wild mammals that live this way rather than living solitary lives? Do human beings have these same benefits and drawbacks? Explain your answer.

Discuss the importance of the author's choice of point of view in "Flowers for Algernon."

There is nothing wrong with the preceding questions except that they are not free-response questions; they are essay questions. They cannot be answered well in two short paragraphs or less, and they require significant thought.

Rule 14 Free-response, short-answer items must be narrow in scope and constructed precisely.

Because such items do not provide answer choices as clues to what you are getting at, you must make this absolutely clear.

Unclear items:

What point does Jonathan Swift make in "A Modest Proposal"?

Swift makes several points that he pretends are advantages to his plan; the parody as a whole makes one quite serious point. What "point" does this question refer to?

What do monkeys and opossums have in common?

These animals have many things in common. Is, for example, "They both have prehensile tails" a sufficient answer? How about "Neither is indigenous to Antarctica"?

How do people react to Charlie's increased intelligence?

Which people? At what point in the story?

Other Issues

If a free-response item is clearly written and sufficiently narrow in scope, deciphering the examinee's handwriting should be the hardest problem you face in scoring. Your key can consist of a series of statements or very short paragraphs, and any paraphrase of what is on the key can be considered correct. However, here, as with any test question, you must remain open-minded. An examinee who provides a good answer *even if it is not the one you were looking for* should be given credit.

While I'm on the subject of credit, let me point out that only a small range is possible with this type of item. Free-response items do allow for some range, unlike multiple-choice, matching, true/ false, and fill-in-the-blank items. For those, an answer is either right or wrong. Period. Free-response slides in the direction of essay in that a range of "rightness" is possible. A partial answer that is accurate as far as it goes could be given one point, a satisfactory but not excellent answer could be given two points, and a thorough and clear answer could be given three points. That's about the limit of the range for this type of item. If you want to make finer distinctions, you're better off using essay questions.

If, however, some short-answer questions are included in a test that also includes a group of multiple-choice or true-false items, you may feel that each short-answer question is worth more than 3 points. If so, you could grade the short-answer questions on a 0-to-3-point scale but double the score you give each item. In any case, it will be important to tell the examinees how many points each question will be worth, so the examinees can gauge the time and effort they wish to give to each question.

CHAPTER 9

ESSAY QUESTIONS

Unlike general guidelines and specific help in how to write a selected-response or short-answer test, for which there is little helpful material available, there is a wealth of useful information readily accessible on the Internet for writing and scoring essay questions. This help ranges in its usefulness, but it is well worth your time to find a source you like and to study it carefully.

Because there is available information elsewhere, and because an in-depth coverage of the subject cannot be dealt with in the scope of a handbook, this chapter will cover only the basics. These basics apply only to essay items used to assess the comprehension of subject matter and the ability to apply that comprehension. The use of essay items to assess writing ability, such as the essays required on statewide tests, is an entirely different matter.

When to Use Essay Items

Essay items provide unparalleled opportunities to assess your students' abilities to interpret, analyze, evaluate, and synthesize material; to problem-solve; and to organize and express their thoughts. If what you're after requires deep and original thought, an essay item is the way to go about getting it.

There are, as stated in Chapter 2, drawbacks to essay items. Not the least among them is the time and effort required to score them, but this is not the only problem. Because writing and scoring good essay questions can be so difficult and because they can be misused, it is important to use them only when they, and only they, are what you need.

Will Another Format Work?

Think carefully about what you want to accomplish with your question because, often, it is possible to achieve it without using a true essay question with its bias in favor of highly verbal students. We all know about Venn diagrams, timelines, and the like, but there are a multitude of graphic organizers that allow students to demonstrate what they know without having to write in complete sentences and well-organized paragraphs. For example:

Think about the contrasting settings—Mason's home and his school—in this story. In the appropriate boxes below, identify a vivid image associated with each place, the overall mood of each place, and what each place symbolizes in the story.

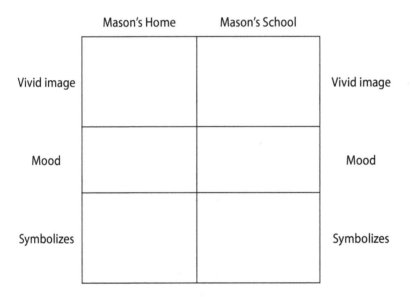

This type of chart, with varied numbers of columns and rows, could be used to name the similarities and differences between Jamestown and Williamsburg, to show the reasons behind any number of wars, to demonstrate familiarity with various scientists and their discoveries or inventors and their inventions, and so on. Students could be asked to rank their entries in order of importance (in answer to a question about, for example, scientists and their discoveries) with another blank column of boxes available for the reason or reasons behind such ranking.

Graphic organizers have the additional advantage of providing a certain level of built-in organization. There are times when you want to test a student's ability to think deeply or to write clear, well-organized paragraphs. There are other times when you just want to test what the student knows about the subject. In the last case, a graphic organizer may be better than an essay question.

Rule 15 Use an essay question only when another format cannot be used for your assessment purpose.

Should You Provide a Choice of Essay Topics?

It is probably better not to. Although it may seem fairer to provide students with a choice of essay questions, it is highly questionable whether doing so is a good idea. For one thing, it is almost impossible to control differences in difficulty among the choices. The student who feels that he or she has more to say in response to one than another may end up choosing to answer what is, in reality, a significantly harder question.

In addition to problems involved in controlling for difficulty level, the scorer of such an array of essays cannot help but compare apples with oranges. Fairly scoring essay questions is hard enough when all the answers are answers to the same question; when they're answers to different questions, it becomes next to impossible.

Provide Specifics

It is important to tell the students exactly what you expect from them and how much time (at least in approximate terms) you expect them to spend on a question. It is also appropriate to let the examinees know the maximum number of points that each question can receive. This is especially true if essay questions are included on a test with items of another type, such as multiple-choice or true/false. It is only fair that students should have a basis for deciding how to distribute their time and effort on the different sections of the test.

You must also let students know if you will be scoring, even in part, based on grammar, mechanics, and spelling. Because you can't begin to score an essay answer you can't read, it is always a good idea to point out that legibility of the response is required.

Scoring the Responses

It is important to remove any biases. A good student may not automatically do better in an individual essay response than a poor student. If it is at all possible for you to hide from yourself who wrote which answer (scramble the test papers? cover the name on the name line?), do so. If it is not—if, for example, you know the students' handwriting too well—try, as best you can, to ignore that knowledge.

It is not always the most facile writer who provides the best response to an essay question; however, the skillful writer has a huge advantage over the less skillful writer. Many an essay seems, when read quickly or superficially, to be much better than it actually is. If you intended to assess your students' ability to problem-solve or to think deeply and creatively about an issue, try not to ignore indications showing that is precisely what they're doing, even if they are expressing themselves poorly. Go ahead and deduct points (if you've told the students you will be doing so) for grammatical, mechanical, and spelling errors, but don't let the fact of such errors keep you from perceiving the thought behind the expression.

Do not claim a wider range of scoring than is actually possible. If you cannot discriminate between an 18-point answer and a 20-point answer, reduce the range. Fine distinctions are worthless if they're not valid.

Creating a Model Response

Try answering any essay question you write by preparing a model response or model responses. You need not write out your answer. Instead, use a list of "checkpoints" that you hope to see in the best responses. You can then more easily, and fairly, grade the students' responses in terms of how many of your checkpoints they include. For example:

Why was Joseph Lister's work successful and important? Include as many details as possible.

- He expanded on earlier work that led to the discovery of the existence of microbes.

- He expanded on earlier work about the "germ theory of disease."

- His experiments proved some diseases are caused by dangerous microbes.

- He formed a theory about the high rate of death from infection among surgical patients.

- He put his ideas into practice by washing his hands and cleaning surgical instruments.

- Death rates at his hospital fell significantly.

- He lectured widely to promote his ideas among resistant doctors.

- His ideas spread beyond operating rooms to affect our daily lives.

Do you think that Sir Lancelot would make a good king? Why or why not?

Students who say yes might point out that:

- He is highly skilled in military matters, so he could defend his people.

- He follows the chivalric code, so he would defend the weak.

- His code of honor would guide his decisions.

Students who say no might point out that:

- He needs to search for adventure and could not be happy with castle life.

- He is too quick to start a fight.

- He would prefer the excitement of battle over the boredom of peace.

Of course, your list of checkpoints can be as long and as detailed as is necessary to suit your purposes. The important thing is that, before you look at even one test paper, you have a clear idea of what a good answer will contain. A facile answer written in excellent prose will not snow you. And a thoughtful answer written in awkward sentences will be easier to recognize. (You must, of course, be flexible. It is entirely possible that one or more students may think of a valid point that you failed to consider.)

Writing model responses accomplishes another very important purpose. It is a way to check that your question can actually be answered and that it tests what you want it to. It's very easy to write essay questions, but not so easy to write good ones. You may write a question that is too broad to be answered well in the space and time provided. Or you may write a question that can be answered in two sentences when you're looking for a longer and more extensive answer. Model responses will signal these problems.

A Potentially Useful Variation

If, for example, you want to see whether your students can recognize illogical reasoning, popular misconceptions, or the like, you might consider having them react to a mock essay by correcting it, providing more (or better) support for the position taken, refuting it, and so forth.

CHAPTER 10

IN REVIEW

The Rules

It might help to have all the rules in one place for a quick refresher:

Rule 1:   Make the task of taking the test as simple as possible.

Rule 2:   Use the item format most appropriate for assessing what you want to assess.

Rule 3:   When the directions say to select one answer, provide one and only one correct answer among the choices.

Rule 4:   Write the stem of a multiple-choice item in such a way that the knowing examinee could write the desired answer on a blank line following it.

Rule 5:   Include no answer choice that includes any other answer choice.

Rule 6:   Incorrect answer choices should function as distractors. They should appeal to examinees who do not have the knowledge or skill that the item requires.

Rule 7:   All items must be discrete, that is, independent of each other.

Rule 8:   Keep your language simple and clear.

Rule 9:   Construct alternate-response items so that it is clear what you are asking about or getting at.

Rule 10: Signal the concept being questioned.

Rule 11: Construct homogeneous lists for matching items.

Rule 12: Construct fill-in-the-blank and completion items so that they have only one correct answer.

Rule 13: In fill-in-the-blank items, omit only significant words from the statement.

Rule 14: Free-response, short-answer items must be narrow in scope and constructed precisely.

Rule 15: Use an essay question only when another format cannot be used for your assessment purpose.

The Purpose of Assessment

Tests have one purpose and one purpose only: to discriminate among levels of knowledge or skill or problem-solving ability or some similar thing in order to determine the level each student has attained.

A test can be as easy or as difficult as you want it to be (as long as no selected-response item is so difficult that the chance factor is greater than the p-value), but the *task of taking the test* must be made as simple as possible. This principle affects every aspect of test development.

In line with this principle is the need to consider the divergent thinker. To avoid problems, never include "distractors" that are *almost* correct. The keyed response must be clearly correct to the knowing examinee, and the distractors must be clearly wrong to that same person.

General Guidelines

Use a selected-response format, usually multiple-choice, only for questions that have definite answers. Using the phrase "best answer" or "best response" does not alleviate the item writer's responsibility for constructing an answer choice, and only one answer choice, that is clearly correct.

Get to the heart of the issue, whatever it is. What fact or detail or understanding is important? That's the one you should be asking the student about. Never test minutiae.

Keep items independent of each other. Not only does this involve never testing the same fact twice, it also means never giving away the answer to one question in the stem of another.

No item should ever involve a complication (reading level, unfamiliar terminology, etc.) that interferes with its ability to test what it purports to test.

Try It

OK, let's see whether you can spot the flaws in the following items. The answers follow the set of items but aren't written upside down, so you might not want to check your ideas until you've finished going through all the items.

Circle *True* or *False*.

1. The first English settlers in the New World arrived in 1607 and founded a settlement at Jamestown in what is now Virginia.   True   False

Fill in the blank.

2. The Battle of Concord was fought in _____.

Circle the letter of the best answer.

3. In the United States, appropriation bills must be introduced by a member of

A. the Senate.
B. the Congress.
C. the House of Representatives.
D. the Executive Branch of the government.

Do the necessary calculations to arrive at the correct answer.

4. You need to bring 8 pounds of fruit salad containing equal amounts of bananas, peaches, watermelon, and oranges to a gathering. How much will you spend if bananas are $.69 a pound, peaches are $1.79 a pound, watermelon is $.49 a pound, and oranges are $1.19 a pound?

Circle the letter of the pair of words that best completes the analogy.

5. pony : horse ::

A. wheels : car
B. sedan : SUV
C. doll : toy
D. tricycle : bicycle

On the line in front of each president's name, write the letter of the war with which he is associated.

6.

_____ James Madison		A. Civil War	
_____ James Polk		B. World War II	
_____ Abraham Lincoln		C. War of 1812	
_____ William McKinley		D. Mexican War	
_____ Franklin Roosevelt		E. Spanish-American War	

Circle the letter of the best answer.

7. Which of the following is a type of poetry?

A. Ode
B. Haiku
C. Sonnet
D. All of the above

Circle *True* or *False*.

8. An amoeba is NOT a living creature.   True   False

Circle the letter of the best answer.

9. In *To Kill a Mockingbird,* Atticus tells Jem never to shoot at mockingbirds because they are

A. harmless.
B. small and easy to miss.
C. dangerous when angered.
D. symbolic of the United States.

Circle the letter of the best answer.

10. In order for a will to be legally binding, it must be

A. fair to all the heirs.
B. witnessed by all the heirs.
C. at least two pages in length.
D. signed by the person whose will it is.

Try It Answers

1. Is the statement true or false? To know, the examinee would have to guess about what is asked. What should the examinee think about? The year, the name of the settlement, the location of the settlement, or the word *first*? In fact, the statement is false. Jamestown was the first *permanent* English settlement, not the first English settlement. (Remember the Colony of Roanoke?) The true/false item needs to be more focused. Let's say you've emphasized the idea that Jamestown was the first permanent English settlement, and you want to know whether your students were paying attention. The following would focus their attention on what you want to know: "The settlement at Jamestown in 1807 was the first attempt by English settlers to found a colony in the New World."

2. In what? In Massachusetts? (If so, what's wrong with "in Concord"?) In 1775? In an effort on the Patriots' part to resist British power? Remember, make the task of taking the test as easy as possible. In this case, that means identifying what is desired by adding "the year" or "the colony of" or whatever is necessary to let the examinee know what that is.

3. There are two right answers. B and C are both correct. The fact that Congress consists of both the Senate and the House of Representatives does not mean that choice B is incorrect. It is important to avoid having any answer choice that subsumes any other answer choice.

4. The stem of this item suggests a falsity and makes a solution to the problem impossible. Unless banana skins, peach pits, watermelon rind, and orange peels are meant to be part of this particular fruit salad, the question is unanswerable.

5. Analogies are wonderful ways to test higher-order thinking skills, but only if there is one specific relationship between the first two items that can be identified. In the case of this particular example, there is not. All of the answer choices are correct. A *pony* and a *horse* can be considered synonyms just as *wheels* and *car* are synonyms in slang. A *pony* is smaller than a *horse* just as a *sedan* is smaller than an *SUV*. A *pony* is a type of *horse* just as a *doll* is a type of *toy*. A *pony* is more appropriate than a *horse* for younger riders just as a *tricycle* is more appropriate than a *bicycle* for younger riders. Every item on every test must have one, and only one, correct answer.

6. The problem here is that there are fewer distractors than the item writer intended there to be. Lincoln's association with the Civil War is part of the nation's consciousness. Franklin Roosevelt is the most recent of the listed presidents, and World War II is clearly the most recent of the listed wars. Even if one isn't sure exactly where Madison falls in the order of the presidents, he is widely known to be an early president, and 1812 was quite an early year in the United States' history as a nation. This leaves only two matches worth testing, not the five the item writer thought were present. This could be fixed by listing the wars in the left column, adding more presidents to the other column (more than there are wars), and rewriting the direction line to fit.

7. First of all, if there is an "All of the above" choice for an item, it had better be a choice for other items as well. A more serious problem is that if the examinee knows that two of the answers are a type of poetry, he or she will be convinced D is the correct response.

8. Never use a negative in a true/false item. There is no reason to do so, and it violates the "make the task of taking the test as easy as possible" rule in spades. It would be just as simple to word this as "An amoeba is a living creature," which makes the item clear.

9. There are really no distractors. B would be true for many, if not most, birds. C is patently ridiculous. D is flawed in two ways: *Symbolic* is a word that may be too difficult for the age group being tested on this particular book, and virtually everyone knows that the eagle is the bird symbolic of the United States.

10. How much do you know about the legal aspects of wills? Still, you had no problem identifying D as the correct answer, right? It makes no sense to include wrong answers that wouldn't distract anyone with even the most cursory knowledge of wills. Remember, the point of any test is to discriminate between the knowing and the unknowing examinee.